BUSTER'S DOG TRAINING AND OTHER STORIES

JENNY BALSDON

Copyright © 2020 by Jenny Balsdon. Published by Seagull Press, Cornwall.

All rights reserved.

No part of this book may be reproduced in any form or by any electronic or mechanical means, including information storage and retrieval systems, without written permission from the author, except for the use of brief quotations in a book review.

I would like to dedicate this book in memory of BUSTER, a friend's lovable Jack Russell. He really was not as naughty, as my book portrays him to be!

ALL ABOUT BUSTER

WOOF! WOOF! I'm a young brown-eyed Jack Russell terrier called BUSTER.

I live with my best-for-ever human friend, Sarah, and her family in Bude, Cornwall.

ALL ABOUT BUSTER

My favourite pastimes are playing FOOTIE, and chasing anything that moves!

I live life to the full – FOOD, FROLIC and FUN!

I seem to cause trouble in whatever I get up to.

Keep reading – and you'll soon find out!

CONTENTS

BUSTER AT THE DONKEY SANCTUARY

1. TROUBLE A-FOOT! — 3
2. MAYHEM IN THE OLDIES BARN — 7
3. MORE FUN AND CARROTS! — 9
4. OUT OF THE DOG HOUSE! — 12

BUSTER'S DOG TRAINING

1. GUESS WHO'S GOING TO DOG TRAINING CLASSES? — 17
2. HELP! I'M IN TROUBLE AGAIN! — 20
3. ALL WORK AND NO PLAY! — 23
4. AM I GOING TO BE A GOOD OR BAD BOY? — 26
5. I'M NOW A VERY GOOD BOY! — 28

CARNIVAL

1. HELP! I'M IN TROUBLE AGAIN! — 33
2. MY BIG DAY ARRIVES! — 36
3. READY! STEADY! GO! — 39

About Jenny, the author — 47
Thank yous — 49

BUSTER AT THE DONKEY SANCTUARY

1
TROUBLE A-FOOT!

I was so excited when I saw we had arrived at the Donkey Sanctuary. There were donkeys everywhere. Well, it was a Donkey Sanctuary after all! They all seemed to have coloured collars around their necks, and I wondered why. I decided I would ask Sarah about this later on.

As soon as the car door opened, I leapt out and ran to the other end of the car park, with Sarah running and chasing me. This was FUN – FUN – FUN – no leash!

Sarah caught up with me, and told me that I was a BAD BOY. I didn't like that one bit. She re-attached my leash, and pointed to the sign which said that all dogs had to be on leads while at the Sanctuary. OK! OK! I had to walk at her pace, because she stopped every few steps to admire the donkeys – BORING!

Suddenly I heard a couple of loud HEE-HAWS! What on earth was that noise?

There it was again. It sounded like something rusty needing oiling.

I looked up to Sarah – WOOF?

"It's only their donkey language to each other." What a relief! When I heard it again, I didn't feel startled or scared anymore.

Ahead, I noticed a large building with big windows with a play area in the front. Sarah told me that this was the Elisabeth Svendsen Trust Centre for children and donkeys, providing riding for children with special needs.

These donkeys were key members of their riding therapy team, and also Adoption Donkeys. I wasn't sure what that meant, but nodded my head as if I'd understood.

I could see their photos attached to the fence, so Sarah told me their names and details. I thought you'd like to know too, so then you'll be as wise as me!

First name on the board was Tom Harrison, a handsome skewbald gelding, who apparently liked playing "FOOTIE" when he had the chance, so I hoped we could have a game together later on.

Next was Daniel P, who was a grey roan gelding, a large and loveable donkey, who loved his ears being tickled and stroked. He had a dreamy look in his eyes, and I wondered what he was thinking about.

Then there was Tapestry, a pretty and gentle skewbald mare, looking quite inquisitive as to whether there was anyone around with a carrot or a ginger nut biscuit for her. She looked quite playful too.

Finally, there was Marguerite who was a pretty light brown mare, and loved her face being stroked. Apparently she is quite cheeky, and quite fast on her feet, as she liked to be the first one out of her stable in the morning, so the others made sure to keep out of her way. Sarah patted Marguerite's face lovingly.

All of a sudden, I spotted a rather squashed and dented black-and-white football in the donkeys' yard, so quick as a flash, I jumped through the wooden bar fence, and made off in its direction, lead dangling from my collar. It was a miracle I didn't get tangled up.

I'd no sooner got my paws on it, than Tom Harrison surged forward, scattering the other startled donkeys, making sure I wouldn't get a chance to play FOOTIE with him. What a spoilsport. I expect he thought – who's this trying to play with MY special ball? But I managed to get my paws on it again, and with my nose I sent it flying down the other end of their enclosure. I love FOOTIE, and I was hoping to show off my FOOTIE skills. We all chased around for a while, until one of the lady grooms grabbed hold of me, quite roughly, held me up in the air and shouted out, "Whose dog is this?"

I tried to wriggle free, but her grip stayed firmly on me.

Sarah was embarrassed, as her face was bright red and she said quietly – "He's mine." Oh dear, I got told off yet again and Sarah too, for not hanging on to my lead.

I was delighted when later we went inside the building to see all the donkeys walking around the enclosure with their young riders, who wore safety helmets, with helpers on either side of them, which they all seemed to be enjoying. When the rides were over, the donkeys and riders went in single file outside. Where to, I didn't know.

In another direction were more stables and donkeys. One was fairly near the fence, and I was told her name was Megan. She was grey in colour and BIG.

I noticed some of their collars, some yellow, and some red. Sarah told me that one states their name and date of birth, and the other is to do with their diet. So now I know and you do too.

Funny to think of donkeys on a diet, isn't it?

"Oh look, there's a Donkey Hospital over there, for poorly donkeys," exclaimed Sarah.

I supposed donkeys got sick sometimes, but what they got sick about, I had no idea. Do you?

2
MAYHEM IN THE OLDIES BARN

Next, we went to the Oldies Barn, where Sarah told me that some of the donkeys were forty years old or more and needed care and attention. Some were eating lots of hay, and completely ignored me by having their backs to me. I thought this was very rude, especially as I'd come to see them all and get more acquainted. Still, the bales of hay looked quite inviting, so in a moment of madness, I leapt through the rails, almost dragging Sarah with me, until I felt her letting go of the leash. It was a great feeling rolling around in that hay! The donkeys were none too pleased, as they made a quick exit, into their yard. I followed them, just as some children opened the outside gate which led into a large field. I pushed it wider with my nose, and made a dash for it, trying to avoid people, children, dogs and donkeys on the way.

I had a fantastic time, chasing here, there and everywhere, causing an uproar and totally ignoring the frantic shouts from Sarah and passers-by.

Panting, I sat down to get my breath back. Should I keep going, or should I go back to Sarah?

Back to Sarah it was then, as I sheepishly made my way back to her in the main yard, which used to be a shippon for cattle, which is really a cowshed. Aren't I the knowledgeable one?

There were pictures of various donkeys around the yard, with their names on. Sarah told me that one picture said, "This donkey loves cuddles," so Sarah put her arms around him, and did just that with a look of bliss on her face. I said to him, "Hey! Hang on a minute, she's mine!"

"You're not the only one to like cuddles you know," replied the donkey. I felt very hurt and resentful that Sarah should prefer a donkey to me. After all, I thought she was my best-for-ever friend.

Suddenly, Sarah turned her attention to me. "I've got enough love for both of you," she said, laughing at the expression on my face. That was alright then, thank goodness. Looking around, I saw a cockerel and hens relaxing on the stone steps. I knew it was a cockerel, because it kept going, "Cock-a-doodle-do!" They must have been used to people walking around them, as they didn't move, much to my relief.

3

MORE FUN AND CARROTS!

Sarah noticed the Information Centre sign, and wanted to go in, and see all the books, donkey novelties, and to enquire about adopting a donkey. What would Sarah want with a donkey when she's got me? Between you and me, I was fed up with all this donkey talk.

Sarah inquired at the desk, and was given an application form and a leaflet about each of the donkeys. Also in the shop, were three other children asking about donkey adoptions. My ears pricked up, and I heard the lady explaining to them that lots of people could adopt the same donkey. They would all receive a photo of their donkey, with a certificate confirming their adoption for a year.

After that, they could renew their adoption, or choose another donkey or even two!

All the adoption fees went towards the donkeys' upkeep for food, bedding and anything else they needed.

So I learned a lot from listening in to their conversations. And now you know too, all about adopting a donkey.

My mind was in a whirl, I can tell you. How would we get it home, and where would it sleep? Hopefully not with me – I didn't fancy sharing MY bed with a donkey! What would it do all day? We didn't even have a field for it to run around in.

While Sarah was shaking out her purse with all her pocket money, I had a quick look around the shop. On the floor was a large basket, which Sarah said was for donated carrots, ginger nuts and polo mints for the donkeys. In my haste, in looking in the basket it tipped over, carrots and polo mints rolling all over the shop floor. There were some more angry shouts, but I escaped through the open door with my prize carrot in my mouth! I waited just outside, below the low wall, where I could see and hear everything, but no one could see me or my carrot! I had several attempts to bite into the carrot, but the bits I tasted were not very nice at all. After that, I abandoned the carrot, leaving it on the ground, with all my teeth marks on it. I returned to Sarah to hear that she had decided to adopt Marguerite.

There was a big grin on Sarah's face. This had made HER day, but definitely NOT mine.

I heard Sarah apologising for my escapade, and watched

her helping to pick up all the scattered donkey food, and put it back in the basket.

I felt a little ashamed of my behaviour, and nudged Sarah beseechingly with my nose. Would she forgive me this time?

Sarah was busy looking lovingly over at Marguerite, and I began to feel sadder than sad.

If Sarah wasn't going to love me any more, then I would NEED to look for someone who would give me a for-ever loving home. I'd miss my comfy bed and my favourite paw-print fleece to snuggle up in, but what option did I have – knowing that she going to prefer to love a donkey instead of me?

I took my time, looking this way and that. There were so many different paths, and where they led to, I had no idea. YES, I was free, but I was feeling miserable. The bottom seemed to have fallen out of my doggy world. I spotted a rabbit, who was hopping from place to place. I gave chase, through a fence, then a gate, but he suddenly vanished out of sight. I sat down to catch my breath. That rabbit sure could run, if you could call it that. Alright – hop!

I chased around and around, each path leading to somewhere unknown, but kept going until I felt quite exhausted. What a huge place. At least if I were a donkey, I'd have a warm and comfy stable to sleep in.

Finding a cosy spot, I snuggled down by a hedge, and fell asleep...

4
OUT OF THE DOG HOUSE!

Suddenly, I heard voices. Was I dreaming? I recognised Sarah's voice – "Buster, there you are by the hedge. I've been so worried about you." Moments later, I found myself scooped up in her arms, and I was being hugged and kissed, again and again!

"I've been looking for you ALL afternoon," she said sternly.

Oh dear, it seemed I would be spending all day in THE DOG HOUSE!

Well, I asked her, "When is the donkey coming, and where will he sleep?"

Laughingly, she explained that the donkey Margurite was a SHE, and would still be living at the Donkey Sanctuary with the others. I was puzzled. The donkey was adopted, but then so was I!

"This is different, Buster. All the adoption money is so that they have lots of money for looking after the donkeys." I was so relieved to find that I wouldn't be sharing my bed with a donkey. I was also over the moon, knowing that I would still have my for-ever home, and YES, Sarah still loved ME, and I was still her best-for-ever friend.

Sarah says I need to go to dog training classes to learn how to be a GOOD boy, but that's another story.

See you again soon!

BUSTER'S DOG TRAINING

1

GUESS WHO'S GOING TO DOG TRAINING CLASSES?

WOOF! WOOF! It's me – Buster. I've got lots to tell you, so you'd better listen.

I'm going to DOG TRAINING CLASSES, apparently to learn how to be a GOOD boy!

Sarah was very excited about it. Half of me was excited, but the rest of me was quite worried about it, so don't tell her I said so will you? Would the other dogs like me, and more importantly, would I like them? Then my hopes rose, as I thought there might be a chance to play "FOOTIE" with them all. How BRILL that would be!

Sarah bought me a new blue collar and lead, which has my name on it. She told me I looked very smart. I agreed, as I caught sight of myself in the hall mirror! What a surprise. I thought for a moment it was my twin brother – silly me!

My BIG DAY had finally arrived! My tummy was trembling a bit, as we set off after tea, with Sarah's dad Jim at the wheel. I sat on Sarah's knee, so that I could see where we were going. In no time at all, we had arrived to find a huge barn, where the Dog Training was held. Jim went in and introduced himself to the trainer, Sally, who welcomed me and Sarah. I noticed that there were five other dogs and their owners waiting to get started, the same as me. Sally introduced everyone, one by one.

First was Trevor with a black-and-white collie named Bertie, then Roger with a beagle named Oliver. Next was Jacky with a springer spaniel named Spot.

Then there was Gemma with a poodle named Bonnie. Nearly to the end now, Andrew with a westie named Star, then finally Sarah with me – Buster! Quite a mixed bunch, don't you think? When I got close to Oliver, he stared at me and growled, which wasn't nice, was it? I was only trying to be friendly, but obviously he didn't want to be friends with me. Oh well, that's his loss, as I know I could be a very good friend.

Sally demonstrated what she wanted each one of us to do with her own labrador puppy – Sasha. SIT-STAY-DOWN-RECALL. What a lot to remember!

They each took their turn, and as I looked around, I didn't see a "FOOTIE" ball anywhere, so I was a bit disappointed in that. I noticed that there were lots of funny shaped things all around the barn. I looked up at Sarah, wondering what they all were.

"It's an obstacle course, Buster," she whispered. I nodded my head, as if I had understood, but I hadn't really. I watched all the others taking their turn. Some took longer than others to get it right. I noticed that when they did get it right, they got a treat! The floor of the barn was covered in sand, so it was nice and soft for my paws to walk on.

2

HELP! I'M IN TROUBLE AGAIN!

Then it was my turn! I can tell you that my tummy was doing somersaults at the prospect. My legs were shaking. Sarah must have noticed, because she bent down and hugged me. That made me feel better.

SIT – yes I did, and got my treat! So far so good. STAY – no, I didn't – and ran over to Sarah. I tried to run off, but she'd tightened my lead, so I couldn't, so I was stuck and so no treat this time. We went over it again and again with Sarah's face getting redder by the minute, so I knew she was very cross with me. Oh dear, if all this was going to make me a GOOD BOY, then I'd rather be a BAD BOY! What do you think?

It wasn't what I imagined it to be like at all. Sarah's lips were in a tight line, and no smiles for me. Right – TRY-TRY-AGAIN. SIT – yes I did and received my treat!

STAY – no I didn't, or should it be wouldn't?

"Come on Buster, try harder, and make me proud of you." This I found was easier said than done! Until I'd got the first two commands right, I couldn't do the other two commands. Dear oh dear, I wish I hadn't come now.

Sally wasn't happy with me either, as she was telling Sarah to practise this at home until the next class. I was feeling really down in the mouth.

Sarah wanted to stay on and watch the Agility Class. These dogs were more experienced apparently and had done their SIT-STAY-DOWN & RECALL correctly.

There were only three in their class, two black-and-white collie dogs and one brown springer spaniel, and boy could they run and jump! This was more like it. How I wished I could join them, as they raced in and out of the tunnels.

All of a sudden, I took one great leap, startling Sarah, and ran across the barn, my lead trailing behind me, and into one of the tunnels and out again, and into another.

This was FUN-FUN-FUN! Sally was shouting at me, which I didn't like one bit. I stayed in one of the tunnels and wouldn't come out! I'd show them who was boss!

All went quiet, so I crept out and decided to jump the fences, but the poles were too high for me, so I went underneath them, and they all came crashing down on the ground, as my back hit them when I jumped. I didn't fancy using the ones that looked like a see-saw. Maybe one of these days I would be a little bit braver.

Sarah was shouting too, and was really red in the face now and angry with me. Oh dear, I was beginning to feel a little ashamed of my behaviour, but I really DID ENJOY doing the Agility. I looked beseechingly at Sarah, and held out my paw to let her know how sorry I was for behaving badly. Would she forgive me?

"What am I going to do with you?" she sighed.

Sally explained to Jim and Sarah that if I didn't behave myself in the future, I could be stopped from coming and learning how to be a GOOD BOY! Sarah agreed to practise teaching me the correct commands every day. I would have preferred to have done the Agility Class first, and the Obedience Class afterwards. What do you think?

So that's DAY ONE over, until the next time. I'll let you know how I get on. I bet you can't wait either, can you?

3
ALL WORK AND NO PLAY!

Sarah promised she would set up some jumps for me to do, if I promised to practice SIT-STAY-DOWN & RECALL. I offered her my paw in reply, which she promptly caught hold of, and kissed my head, and fondled my ears lovingly. I do love being a made a fuss of. It makes me feel all quivery inside and happy.

I was now ready and willing to have another go at it. I hoped she had those treats handy.

"Right Buster, let's get started and let the dog see the rabbit." I turned around, but couldn't see a rabbit anywhere. Puzzled, I looked up at her, questioning. "It's OK Buster, it's just what I hear mum saying sometimes, I'm not sure what it means either!"

SIT – GOOD BOY, and yes I had my treat. STAY – GOOD BOY, and another treat!

DOWN – "NO Buster, LIE DOWN." Alas, no treats this time. We went over it again and again. I was getting a bit bored by now. Oh well, try again, as she pushed my rear to the ground. "That's what DOWN means, Buster. Let's have another go."

Here we go again! Hooray! I finally did it, so got my reward. What a relief!

Then I had to lie down again, until she counted to ten, and called me to come to her. I was having a breather, so didn't bother! I was a BAD BOY again and no treat!

Then I thought if I wanted to do some jumps, then I'd better oblige, which I did. "GOOD BOY," and yes finally I had my treat!

I was barking with happiness, and apparently making such a loud noise, that Sarah's mum came running out, wondering what all the fuss was about.

"He's finally done all his commands mum, and he's telling you all about it," explained Sarah. "Well done Buster, what a GOOD BOY you are."

My chest puffed up with pride. At least I'd done something right today!

I was having a drink from my bowl, when Sarah came running past with two large sandcastle buckets. What was she going to do with those, I wondered?

She turned them upside down, and put a broomstick handle over the top of them, so I could do my jumps. How clever she was to think of that. They were just the right height for me to jump over, without me knocking anything down. As you know, my legs are quite short being a Jack Russell, so this was BRILL!

Every day, we did the same, doing SIT-STAY-DOWN & RECALL and then the jumps, plus all those treats!

4

AM I GOING TO BE A GOOD OR BAD BOY?

It's DOG TRAINING for me again! I'm keeping my paws crossed that things will go well for me tonight. So keep yours crossed for me too, please.

Sally met us at the door, along with her labrador Sasha. She hoped that we had been practising all the commands, which Sarah told her that we had.

So I hope she would see how much we had improved since the last fiasco!

All the ones who were there before, were there again. Oliver still growled at me, so I ignored him. Star the westie must have been having an off day, as he kept getting it wrong, and it was ages before he finally got it right. Last week he did really well for a westie. Bonnie was having an off day too, I guess, as she didn't do as well as she did last week.

I was last again. I expect Sally was saving the best one until last, don't you agree?

Right. SIT – YES – GOOD DOG and my treat, STAY- YES – another treat! DOWN – YES, and a treat, RECALL – NO-NO-NO – BAD DOG.

"Come on Buster, you know you can do it. Do it for me PLEASE!"

I gave myself a little shake, and promptly obliged! GOOD DOG, and got my reward, much to Sarah's delight. "Well done, Buster!"

I'd finally done it, and what a relief it was to get it over and done with.

Sally was pleased with me too for a change, and even Sasha came over to rub noses as if to congratulate me. The others were a bit more aloof, and kept their distance, which didn't worry me in the slightest.

Sarah wanted to stay on again and watch the three dogs doing their Agility Course. She kept a tight hold on me, so I couldn't run off and do what I did last time.

It was thrilling watching them, and half of me wanted to join in, although the other half of me knew I couldn't really compete with them. They were like miniature race horses.

5
I'M NOW A VERY GOOD BOY!

I've now decided that I don't want to join the Agility Class. I've tried DOG TRAINING, and it was fun while it lasted. I'm quite content to do my jumps at home, play "FOOTIE", go for walks with Sarah, ride in the car, and I love my food, biscuits, and of course my best-forever friend Sarah.

I also love my paw-print fleece to snuggle up in my basket, and when no one's looking, I creep up the stairs at bedtime and jump up on the bed beside Sarah. In the morning, I creep downstairs before anyone is up and about and back into my basket! That's our secret, so don't tell anyone else, will you?

I really do like having FUN-FUN-FUN.

Sarah still practices SIT-STAY-DOWN & RECALL with me. I must admit that I'm getting to be an expert at it now. I could probably teach you a thing or two as well. What do you think about that?

I'm just waiting to hear what she'll teach me next. For a dog, I'm very intelligent, but I expect you know that already, don't you?

CARNIVAL

1
HELP! I'M IN TROUBLE AGAIN!

WOOF! WOOF! It's me – Buster. I've got lots more to tell you, so you'd better listen carefully.

Sarah ran up the stairs, and I quickly followed her. Where was she going, and what was she going to do? Ah – her mum's sewing room! Sarah was really excited as her mum was making her an outfit to enter in Bude Carnival. Mary was busy using her sewing machine, which was making a funny whirring noise.

On the floor was a large basket with funny-shaped coloured things in it. I looked up to Sarah with a questioning look. She told me that they were cotton reels for stitching things together. Oh! So now I know, and so do you! I went to take a closer look, and put my paws in the basket, and

WHOOPS – it tipped over, and the cotton reels were rolling all over the floor.

What a tangle, as the reels scattered in all directions. Mary was not best pleased with me, as I noticed by the look on her normally smiling face.

"Oh BUSTER! YOU BAD BOY!" exclaimed Sarah. Me – BAD? I thought I had learnt how to be a GOOD BOY! So this was news to me, and I bet it surprised you too, didn't it?

Knowing I had disgraced myself, I went down the stairs faster than I had come up!

Next morning, I crept up the stairs again and poked my head around the door of Mary's sewing room, and saw that the cotton reels had been sorted out and back in the basket. I didn't dare go in, in case the same thing happened again! I bet you'd stay clear too, if this had happened to you?

This seemed to go on for days, and I thought – how much longer was this sewing going on? It was getting boring, as I liked having FUN-FUN-FUN!

Coming down the stairs one day, I was feeling a bit sorry for myself, as Sarah was upstairs getting excited to see her outfit for the Carnival almost finished.

Oh well, a game of FOOTIE would be good, but after a while, it wasn't much fun playing FOOTIE on my own, as there was no one to kick or throw the ball in my direction. I noticed that my jumps were still on the lawn, with the sandcastle buckets and the broom handle over the top. This was fun for a while, and with still no sign of Sarah, I went indoors and had a drink and a few nibbles left in my bowl, and snuggled up in my paw-print fleece, put my paws over my face and went to sleep.

2

MY BIG DAY ARRIVES!

The day of the Carnival had finally arrived! Sarah's dad Jim had been decorating a trailer, plus a bench for Sarah to sit on, which he had fastened down, for what seemed like weeks. He'd kept the trailer in the shed, and behind closed doors, there was lots of hammering and banging! None of us were allowed a look in, as it was all going to be a surprise! I expect you're wondering too, aren't you? Sarah told me that she was going as Little Red Riding Hood, whoever that is. Do you know? If you do, you can tell me later!

Jim had borrowed a van and had attached the trailer on to the back of it. I must say that the trailer looked really eye-catching, with coloured ribbons, flowers, and a painted woodland scene at the back, with a view of a cottage in the background. Clever old Jim!

Just after 5pm, Jim drove into Bude with the Carnival float, followed by Mary in the car with Sarah and me. I put my paw on her watch, and looked up at her, wondering why we were leaving so early. She told me that at 6pm the roads into Bude would be closed for the carnival procession to go through the town. So now I know, and so do you! I must say she looked really amazing in her red cape over her white sparkly dress. Beside her she had a small basket filled with fruit and flowers. She said they were a present for Granny! Granny who? Oh never mind, I expect she'll tell me later on.

I noticed that everyone was lined up ready and waiting for the judging to be over, so that they could start the procession at 7pm. We waited around for ages and ages, and I started to get bored and impatient. Sarah got out of the car, and on to the trailer and sat on the bench with her basket. I jumped up beside her, but after a while Jim said "No – Buster, you'll be in the van with me." At first I was very disappointed, but then thrilled at having a bird's eye view of everything from the van. I felt like a VIP, that's a Very Important Person – just to let you know!

Jim told me that Sarah had been awarded a 2nd Class Prize Certificate, which she was thrilled about, and so was I! All their efforts had been rewarded.

Sarah begged and begged for me ride on the float with her, until Jim finally relented, much to my relief and Sarah's delight. He told me that I could ride home in the van afterwards, and to be GOOD!

How could I be anything else, seeing as I'd trained to be a GOOD BOY?

3
READY! STEADY! GO!

We all had to wait until it was our turn to proceed. How much longer would we have to wait?

At last! Bude Band were the first to lead the procession, all looking very smart in their blue uniforms, playing their musical instruments as they walked along. I don't know what tune they were playing, but it sounded good. Next came the town's dignitaries. Following them were all the visiting Kings, Queens, Princes and Princesses, and then the Youth Clubs, Play Groups, and I mustn't forget the lovely Majorettes in their bright outfits, displaying their talents. Forgive me if I've missed out any, but I couldn't see everything that was coming along behind us or in front.

Then it was our turn, moving slowly, so crowds of people

lining the streets could get a better view. People, children and dogs were everywhere, all enjoying themselves.

There were walkers all dressed in funny costumes, and people shaking their collecting buckets. Mary was shaking a bucket too, but was near Sarah's float. Children were throwing pennies at the floats, and those that fell on the ground, excited children ran out to pick them up. Loud music, Oohs and Ahhs and cheering filled the evening air. Everywhere I looked people seemed to be eating or drinking!

I was sitting on the bench beside Sarah so had a fantastic view. If I could wave like the Queen, I would have, but paws aren't shaped like hands are they?

We came along the Crescent, and into the Strand, and slowly over the speed bumps.

I turned my head in all directions, so I didn't miss anything. I smiled at everybody – at least I hoped it was a smile! I could feel the warm evening air, and the gentle breeze on my face, fluffing out my ears.

I was getting bored with all the stopping and starting, I can tell you. I expect you would be too, if you were me! I could hear loud music and more walkers dressed in funny costumes, dancing to the beat.

I saw a man holding a handful of large colourful balloons, their streamers hanging down, and blowing in the breeze. This looked interesting, and I jumped off the float, and on to the ground, which was higher than I expected. Luckily for me, I landed on all four paws!

I heard Sarah shouting at me to come back – but the balloons looked so inviting,

I jumped up and caught some of the streamers in my mouth, startling the balloon seller, so several of them went floating high up into the air. I could tell he was not best pleased with me, in fact quite angry, but this was FUN-FUN-FUN! I gave myself a little shake, when suddenly strong hands grabbed hold of me!

People yelled at me, demanding to know who I belonged to. Eventually I was reunited with Sarah, who said "Sorry" to the man.

"Keep a firm hand on him next time, miss!" he replied.

ME? Needing a firm hand? Sarah told me in no uncertain terms, that I was indeed a BAD BOY! How could someone trained to be GOOD, be BAD? I didn't know the answer, and I expect you don't either, do you?

Crowds of people were lining the street as we went up Belle Vue, cheering and clapping. I could smell beefburgers and everywhere I looked people seemed to eating and drinking.

More crowds were up around the Post Office and Morwenna Terrace, all trying to get a better view of the procession. Sarah informed that me that we were now going along Burn View.

On my left I noticed that there were lots of people waving sticks in the air, and pulling things on wheels. WOOF? Sarah replied that they were golfers hitting balls to go into a hole, and wheeling their golf trolleys which held their spare golf clubs. Obviously they were not interested in watching the Carnival. Still, crowds of people were standing around – where had they all come from, I wondered?

Music was still blaring out, and some people were still dancing around in the street to the beat. Then I heard sirens in the distance. Sarah said that they were the Police, Ambulance, and Coastguard, all with flashing lights, and I think that was last of the procession. Now and again I would glimpse the lights reflecting on the other vehicles. I'm very observant, don't you think? I like to know what's going on, and I expect you do too!

We were now coming down Lansdown Road, where lots of people were eating ice creams. My mouth watered at the thought! Vanilla ice cream is my favourite. How about you?

There were still loads of people about cheering and clapping. Lots of them were taking lots of photos, I noticed. I wonder if they had taken any of me on the float? I'm sure I would make a lovely photo, or lots of photos, as I think I'm quite photogenic!

The procession had just come down to the Triangle, where it stopped briefly. People were sitting on the wall surrounding it, to get a better view of us all. Suddenly, I spotted the water fountain in the centre of the Triangle, which looked really tempting! So with another unexpected leap, I found myself on the ground, and yes – on all four paws again and headed for the fountain. Sarah's shouts were ringing in my ears, but I ignored her, and leapt into the fountain. It was great, like being in the shower at home, on the occasions when I'd got really muddy from splashing about in the puddles, but that's another story. The water was lovely, cool and refreshing, so I had a drink too! My excitement however was short lived, as I was grabbed quite roughly, and held up high, soaking wet and dripping from head to paws, as a man said, "Oh, not YOU again!" I was taken back to Sarah in disgrace!

I was made to sit on the floor, as she didn't want to get her outfit wet. She gave me a good telling off, so my ears were red hot!

Back into the Strand again, people were still there waiting to see us all again the second time around.

Then back to the Crescent, from where we had all started out.

That too, seemed to take forever, as everyone was getting themselves sorted out for the journey home. Some of the trailers were now empty, apart from their decorations still intact.

Mary and Sarah were talking to the other competitors, and fundraisers, about the Carnival I suppose. Some people seem to talk forever, don't they? ME? I was still on the float, patiently waiting to go home, and then getting impatient as the talking and waiting continued! If I could have pressed the horn in the van I would have, to hurry things along – TIME TO GO HOME!

But I was so wet, I was not allowed to have my ride home in the van.

As soon as we got home, I went on the lawn and shook all the water off me. It sprayed out in all directions! So now I was just a bit damp. I then went indoors and held out my paw to Sarah to let her know how sorry I was for misbehaving. "You really were a very BAD BOY today Buster, but I love you all the same. You've got to learn how to stay being a GOOD BOY!"

To round off the day, Jim treated us all to a fish and chip supper, which went down a treat, I can tell you. So I knew that I'd been forgiven for being such a BAD BOY! Sarah cut up my portion into small pieces, and I scoffed the lot, then looked expectantly up at Sarah for more. It tasted great with not too much salt or vinegar, the way I like it. "I think you've had enough Buster for now, or you'll burst!" Now that would be messy wouldn't it, and you wouldn't want that to happen, would you?

At home, Jim unhooked the trailer and put it back into the shed.

By this time I was getting sleepy, but my head was still at

the carnival with the floats, the music, balloons and yes the fountain, and me on the float looking out at everything and everybody.

Now I knew what to expect, I was looking forward to next year's carnival, but that was a whole year to wait, and that's a long time for you and me!

With all that going round in my head, I eventually fell asleep snuggled in my paw-print fleece, comforted by the thought that I was still Sarah's best-for-ever friend!

WOOF! WOOF!

ABOUT JENNY, THE AUTHOR

Although Jenny has no pets at present, she is an avid animal lover. She has been adopting donkeys from the Sidmouth Donkey Sanctuary for many years, and visits them regularly.

Jenny sponsors Guide Dog puppies for training as Guide Dogs and Poorly Pets, for owners who can't afford the cost of treating their pet. She loves looking through her albums full of photos of all the animals she has sponsored. Look out for tales of their adventures and escapades in Jenny's future books!

Jenny is also one of the founder members of the Bude Friends Group, fundraising for the Children's Hospice South West, a charity which is very close to her heart. There are three Hospices all caring for children with life-limiting conditions and their families. Jenny has visited all three, most often Little Bridge House at Fremington in Devon.

To share your thoughts on Buster's tales or get in contact with Jenny, email jennybalsdon@talktalk.net Please also tell your friends about Buster and consider leaving a review on Amazon or other online book retailers. These are a huge help to authors!

THANK YOUS

I would like to acknowledge editor and literary consultant Claire Wingfield for inspiring and guiding me, and enabling me get this book published.

My thanks to my illustrator Coralie Jenkins-Packer for the beautiful illustrations and to Jess at The Ricketty Desk for making them into Buster's cover.

And to my loving, ever patient husband Den for supporting me.

www.ingramcontent.com/pod-product-compliance
Lightning Source LLC
Chambersburg PA
CBHW021133080526
44587CB00012B/1266